SPRINTS AND HURDLES

by

Joe Walker
University of Florida

ISBN No. 0-932741-08-8

Cover and drawings by Glenn Amundsen.

ISBN 0-932741-08-8

PRINTED IN THE UNITED STATES OF AMERICA

Championship Books
P.O. Box 1166—ISU Station
Ames, Iowa 50010

SPRINTS AND HURDLES

EDITOR'S NOTE:

To avoid awkward phrasing, the generic pronouns *he, him,* and *his* are used throughout the book. However, *she, her,* and *hers,* can be substituted.

Table of Contents

PREFACE

My concept of sprinting and hurdling is the result of ideas from many sources. I've always tried to read as many books and articles as were available. In addition, I've talked with outstanding athletes and coaches. Also, and probably equally as influential, has been my work with my own athletes. Through our various successes and failures we've found things that just seem to work and things that didn't work or didn't fit our style. You always learn more if you work *with* your athletes. The athletes' feedback is invaluable. I always remind myself of a saying I came across a few years ago that says, "I'd rather have one man working with me than three men working for me." Finally, I have had the pleasure of growing up under a fine track coach—Joe Walker, Sr. During his high school coaching career, he developed many fine athletes and teams, as well as some original ideas that were ahead of his time.

There are many roads to success in virtually every field. What this book attempts to convey is what has worked for me. Hopefully, some of our ideas can be suited to your style and athletes. As in all forms of coaching, a coach must be true to himself and his beliefs.

GENERAL PHILOSOPHY

To properly understand the drills in this book you must have a knowledge of the factors involved in the events. As a coach, once you understand the concept of the events and their respective needs you will be able to see how the drills improve these various factors and which ones to include in your program.

There are two primary concepts that will be discussed in detail. The first concept is applicable to both hurdling and sprinting because hurdling is a sprint race. The other concept applies only to hurdlers. Each of these will be discussed more fully because an understanding of them is essential to proper implementation of the drills. A hurdler should always do much of his work with the sprinters. A maximum of no more than two days per week is specifically designed to hurdle work, although some hurdlers do warm-ups and starts over hurdles virtually every day.

Part I

SPRINT CONCEPTS

PART I
SPRINT CONCEPTS

Sprinting requires a person to overcome inertia, accelerate to maximum speed, maintain top-end velocity and decelerate as little as possible to the finish line. Sprinting is a skill and like any other skill, it can be refined. There are factors that influence how fast a person can run. Some people have more of the factors naturally, while others succeed becuase they are persistent and develop the necessary qualities over a period of time. One of the all-time great sprinters, Valery Borzov, a Russian, was not a great sprinter as a teenager. When we talk of talent, that term usually refers to many variables. The normal law of survival of those who have achieved success usually sorts out athletes as soon as they move from elementary to junior high, junior high to high school, and high school to college racing. Everyone can refine the skill of running faster; but everyone cannot be declared World Class.

Among the factors involved in sprint success are:

A. EXPLOSIVE MUSCLE ORIENTATION/FAST TWITCH FIBERS
B. STRENGTH
C. NEURO-MUSCULAR COORDINATION/TECHNIQUE
D. FLEXIBILITY
E. CONDITIONING
F. START ABILITY
G. MENTAL/PSYCHOLOGICAL APPROACH TO EVENT/LIFE
H. TRAINING

Each of these factors is explained in more detail:

A. EXPLOSIVE MUSCLE ORIENTATION/FAST TWITCH FIBERS
   People are born with certain physiological talents that allow them to excel at certain activities. People who excel in sprinting have a higher percentage of white, or fast-twitch muscle fibers. Training can affect this percentage slightly.

B. STRENGTH
   Strength training is an integral part of training for sprinters. The best method is a combination of free weights and machines. The emphasis and type of lifts vary according to the time during the training year. A proper weight routine is one of the most valuable tools used to improve sprint times. There is a difference in the program between the maximum strength gained through weight lifting done in the weight room and elastic strength that is gained from plyometrics. There is nothing to fear if you exercise all muscles on a limb. This and flexibility training will negate any idea of muscle boundness.

C. NEURO-MUSCULAR COORDINATION/TECHNIQUE
   Neuro-muscular coordination is an important factor in successful sprinting. It is often overlooked and misunderstood.

2

An extremely high level of rhythmic synchronization of neurons is required to induce the muscle to contract and relax at the precise moment. As coaches we talk about the ability to relax during high intensity in terms such as rhythm . . . natural speed . . . smooth running strides . . . and on and on. All of these words and phrases partially describe what is occurring, but none seem to convey the total concept. The "art" of sprint coaching may be directly related to the coach's ability to recognize and teach this concept. Likewise, the athletes natural tendency to execute correctly or his ability to learn. Form problems at high speed (near the end of a 100 meter race) are caused more by a tiring of the nerves than by a tiring of the muscle. The longer the sprint (200,400) the more the fatigue becomes a product of energy expenditure and not neurological fatigue.

Tommie Smith

Valery Borzov

Film Footage of Tommie Smith and Valery Borzov.

D. FLEXIBILITY
Research and years of practical coaching prove that improved flexibility will allow the muscles to move more freely through a full range of motion. There simply is no tightness to inhibit the muscle as it performs. It also helps prevent injuries. An elaborate warm-up routine should be used. Athletes should be encouraged to stretch during the post workout and race warm-down. Flexibility can be dramatically improved.

E. CONDITIONING
All coaches should be aware of the law of specificity. Our bodies adapt in a precise and specific way to the activity. Conditioning for sprinting is primarily anaerobic. In the sprints, there are two primary systems used to produce energy. The first six to nine seconds are the ATP-PC system. The longer sprints (10-70 seconds) combine the ATP-PC system with the LA system. Any conditioning of the oxygen (aerobic) system does not affect sprint performance. What it does do and why it is necessary,

is it allows the body to recover more efficiently and quickly. This effects recovery between workout segments and the ability to recover between workouts and races.

EVENT	PERCENTAGE OF ENERGY CONTRIBUTION		
	ATP-PC (Short Sprint Work)	LA Lactic Acid Build-up Work	O^2 Aerobic—Oxygen System Work
100 meters	85%	10%	5%
200 meters	52%	28%	10%
400 meters	22%	55%	22%

F. START ABILITY

The start is a separate skill that must be learned and incorporated into the other skills for a person to be a top level short sprinter (60 to 100 meters). It is also important in the longer sprints.

The primary purpose of learning the starting skill is to overcome inertia and gain the most from the early acceleration phase. A look at the starts of the great sprinters shows as many variations as it does similarities. As with virtually all phases of track and field coaching, mechanical principles must not be ignored but must be individualized.

Bob Hayes '64 Olympic Champion

Valery Borzov '72 Olympic Champion

Sprinters should use a variation of the medium or elongated start that feels comfortable to them. As a general rule, the front foot is about 24 inches behind the starting line. If placed down, the lead knee would rest on the line. Actually, look for a 90 degree angle in the set position of the front leg. The back leg should have an angle of 120 to 135 degrees. These angles and a comfortable feeling dictate the height of the hips.

The athlete is comfortably tense in the blocks, much like a coiled spring. At the gun, he pushes with both legs. However many coaches try to teach the concept of a power side—the front foot—and a quick side. The movement of the back leg and the opposite arm creates more force into the front leg block because of action-reaction law. The athlete must come out powerfully and drive each stride into more and more speed. He will not pop up, but neither will he stay down. Drive! . . . and get into good sprint form as soon as possible. On the first stride the foot must land inside the knee for proper balance and acceleration position. Just as important as the mechanics of the start, is the philosophy. The idea of the start is not to be the first out of the blocks or even first at 30 yards. A clear understanding of the acceleration phase of the sprint is a must. If a person clears the blocks too quickly, he cannot create enough force for a long fast acceleration phase. After a powerful drive from the blocks, each stride is slightly longer than the previous one and the velocity increases. Maximum velocity should occur between 50 and 65 meters.

A person who doesn't create the necessary force from the blocks and during the early acceleration phase (by body position), will reach maximum "leg turn over" too quickly. This will create too long a phase where he is "trying to maintain and decelerate the least possible." The sprinter must store power during the early acceleration phase and key on quickness, leg turn over, and maintenance during the later stages. Early in the race the foot contacts the ground longer and create more and more power resulting in acceleration from zero to increasing speeds.

At this point the athlete is functioning at the perfect combination of stride frequency and stride length. When this occurs, the foot is in contact with the ground for only a short time and maintenance of that speed is all that is left. Continued acceleration is impossible because of the short contact phase. Here is a graphic look at the race:

Clear Blocks	Accelerate To Full	Maintain	Decelerate
10 meters	50 meters	70 meters	100 meters

Another way to look at the race is the percentage of contribution each phase has to the total time. Most authorities seem to view it as:

Reaction and Block Clearance	6%
Acceleration to full speed	64%
Ability to maintain full speed	18%
Deceleration phase	12%
	100%

All of these areas can be improved, but the maintenance and deceleration phases seem to be the areas where proper coaching can yield the greatest gains.

G. MENTAL AND PSYCHOLOGICAL APPROACH TO EVENT AND LIFE

When talking about success and winning, we must always include the mental and psychological area as a key factor. In all areas of life, we find slightly less-endowed people succeeding. Talent and natural intelligence have never been valid predictors of who will succeed. In sprint coaching, emphasize and recognize this factor. One of the difficulties about improving sprint times is the small margin of improvement available. An improvement is usually in hundredths of seconds instead of minutes and full seconds. This always creates possible problems in the confidence of a sprinter and in his enthusiasm about the training program. Since sprinting is a series of upsetting the center of mass and consequent recovery, there is also a fear factor in fast sprinting. The athlete must be geared to maintain poise and confidence in spite of the tension and closeness of a race. All big races will be close and being prepared for this mentally, without creating fear, can be the small factor that makes the difference. Looking around and worrying about others in the race does no good. The illustrations below show the small margin of victory. The winner has been able to focus on himself and the task at hand rather than become overwhelmed worrying about all the others in the race.

Try to expose your sprinters early to the mental pressures involved. They must learn to lose—able to cope with defeat without faking an injury or making excuses. The only thing to do with a loss is to look at the mistakes and go back resolved to do better.

H. TRAINING

Training should be a correct blend of activities to improve the above factors according to an individual's needs. Training is more than what a person does at the track or in the weight room. It embodies a life style. Training is a form of stress. Improvements take place when the organism (person: mind/body) adapts to that stress. A review of the ideas of Hans Seyle and his view of stress is important. We should also realize that our adult lives are ruled by the habits we've created. Therefore, all training should focus on the creation of good habits. This applies to our mechanical-movement habits as well as our personal life style habits.

Obviously, specificity must be applied to the sprints in terms of training. To begin with, however, all of our sprinters are grouped as 100-400 men. There are more things in common for the 100-200 up to the 400 than there are differences. Begin training them in all the elements of the three groups. Only after an athlete shows outstanding talent in either the short sprints or the longer sprints should he specialize. This keeps with the overall teaching philosophy of moving from general to specific. Ideally, all training and coaching should progress from:

slow to fast
easy to difficult
quantity to quality

It is important to race slightly over and under an athlete's main event. This creates a training effect that cannot be reproduced in practice. All of the training is an attempt to improve each of the factors mentioned earlier. The blend of these depends on the individual athlete. No attempt is made to give weekly workouts in this book—only guidelines and concepts. Here is a general outline of the yearly sprint plan and its objectives:

FALL

* Begin teaching the program philosophy
* Mental toughness—ability to push yourself and adjust to problems
* Strength, flexibility, endurance
* Lots of drill work and plyometrics

WINTER

* Begin to do more "competitive" type training
* Interval runs are #1 in importance
* Starts and some relay work
* Continue drills, weights and plyometrics

COMPETITIVE

* Specialize more—specific to event
                    specific to individual needs
* Quality and rest are key words
* Starts, accelerations, varied speed work
  M/W—overdistance & stress
  T/TH—speed, relay, specialty, weights

Part II

HURDLE CONCEPTS

PART II
HURDLE CONCEPTS

After realizing they are sprinters first, hurdlers must understand the concept of balance. The hurdlers should sprint and clear the hurdles quickly and with as much balance as possible. Hurdle clearance is simply an exaggerated sprint stride. To clear the hurdle with proper balance the athlete must understand hurdle technique.

A. HURDLE TECHNIQUE

APPROACHING THE HURDLE:
1. Run with normal sprint technique.
2. Stay tall and lead with the knee while driving off the toe.
3. Drive the opposite arm out and slightly across the body's mid-line.
4. Begin by teaching a 1½ arm thrust. Don't, however, be opposed to using a double arm or a single arm thrust if the athlete adapts better to these than the preferred 1½ arm thrust.

ATTACKING THE HURDLE:
1. As the athlete becomes air-borne, he should drive forward with the upper body.
2. A good key to look for is that the chin is directly over the knee and the chest is very close to the lead leg's thigh.
3. The lead foot should point forward and clear in the middle of the hurdle. The whole body should remain "squared" to the track.

4. The trail leg does not pull through immediately. In good technique there is a wide split between the lead leg and the trail leg. The active drive of the lead leg and the forward drive of the upper body creates the split.

5. After the explosive toe drive from the ground, the trail leg should slightly "toe out." This opens the hip and allows for a smoother, quicker trail leg action.

ON TOP OF THE HURDLE:
1. Maintain the chin over the knee.
2. The lead arm begins to sweep back and down. The wrist should always stay below the elbow.

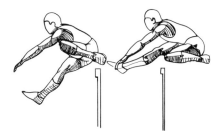

3. The trail leg is pulled or snapped through quickly. The trail leg arch goes from flat to high under the arm pit.

4. The actual clearance looks like the illustration below. The position that looks like the "hurdler's stretch" comes before clearance.

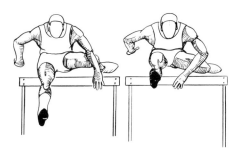

COMING OFF THE HURDLE:

1. The upper body releases the extreme forward lean and **slightly** snaps up just as the trail leg and buttocks area clears the hurdle.
2. The action of the trail leg pulling through, and the slight upper body rise, cause the lead leg to snap down and make ground contact quicker.

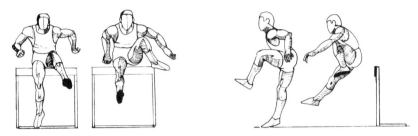

3. The trail leg must come through quickly and continue on to a normal length sprint stride. Many young hurdlers make the mistake of dropping the trail leg off the hurdle. This creates an extremely short stride.
4. The upper body maintains enough lean so that it is in front of the center of mass on landing. Landing should be made on the toes. We often say "sprint into the lean."
5. The arm that has been beside the hip and used for balance should be moved in normal sprinting fashion quickly to the chin.

B. INTERMEDIATE HURDLE TECHNIQUE

Technique over the hurdles is not as important as in the high hurdle race. Balance, rhythm, step pattern, and conditioning are the keys for the 400-meter hurdles. The basic technique concepts are the same as for the high hurdles.

Because the intermediate hurdles aren't as high, the center of mass isn't raised as much. This means the lean of the upper body is not as necessary. Balance and getting back into 400 sprint form are the keys to good technique.

1. Stay tall—don't drive into the hurdle until air-borne. Lead with the knee and drive off the toes.

2. This position is similar to the high hurdles except the chest does not fold down into the lead leg—there isn't much upper body lean.

3. The trail leg comes through slightly flatter in the intermediates than in the highs. It is still important to bring it through high enough to insure a long, fluid first stride off the hurdle.

A similar concept that applies to hurdle technique is that there is a difference between leg speed and quickness. Leg speed refers to the athlete's sprint ability and is improved through normal 100- and 200-sprint training. Quickness refers to the technique over the hurdle and is developed through constant drilling of correct technique.

Throughout the book you'll find drills that will improve each of the concepts mentioned in the introduction.

Part III

DAILY WORKOUT PATTERNS

PART III
DAILY WORKOUT PATTERN

Each workout should have four separate phases, all of which are important. It is often the little things that separate winners and losers. Luck favors the prepared mind and body. Benjamin Franklin made a valid statement when he said "by failing to prepare, you are preparing to fail."

1. WARM-UP: This prepares the body for the coming stresses of the main work-out. Start with easy jogging to raise the pulse level and the muscles inner temperature. Then do static stretches. The next segment is sprint drills. After the jogging, stretching and drills, take a 5-minute break to go to the bathroom. You are now ready for the main work-out.

2. ACTUAL WORK-OUT: This is the main part of the day. This varies from day to day, week to week.

3. STRENGTH PHASE: It is best to follow most main work-outs with a strength phase. This takes the form of explosive jump drills called plyometrics, or of strength work in the weight room. Vaulters also use the gymnastic room. Sometimes do sprint drills again during this period.

4. WARM-DOWN: The final phase is the warm-down period. Too often this is neglected. As the body moves into the hard work-out at a slower pace, the body returns to normal after a hard work-out. Research has proved that a warm-down consisting of jogging, walking, and stretching will reduce the amount of lactic acid in the muscles and aid recovery from work-out to work-out. The warm-down should only take about 10 minutes and be a smaller version of the warm-up.

It is wise for the athlete to use a date book and record the actual daily work-outs. This allows the coach and athlete to see what works and to compare work-outs from year to year.

Part IV

DRILLS FOR
SPRINTS AND HURDLES

DRILLS FOR THE SPRINTS AND HURDLES

Flexibility Drills

The improvement and maintenance of flexibility is critical to all sprinters and hurdlers. There are many flexibility drills one can use. An excellent book on flexibility is *Stretching* by Bob Anderson.

In flexibility drills, it is important to realize that all stretching should be done slowly and gradually. The majority of stretches should be static. Stretch the muscle to a point of tightness that still feels comfortable. Hold this position for a count of 15. Relax and repeat. The key to improved flexibility is to be consistent. A gradual, comfortable stress through moderate stretching will yield improved flexibility. Each week the point of tightness should change just a little. Below are some examples of possible flexibility drills:

1) **Toe Touch:** Place ankles together, lock knees, and bend over toward toes.

2) **Saigon Stretch:** Heels stay on ground. Squat down and hold that position.

3) **Stride Out:** Simply execute a long stride out and hold. Then, reach back and pull ankle back toward buttocks.

4) **Side Stretch:** Sway from side to side with a gentle stretch.

5) **Split:** This is done from a sitting position. Separate legs and lower upper body into the open area between them.

6) **Pretzel:** Place left leg across the right leg in bent knee fashion. Then, twist upper body to the left and hold position.

7) **Hurdle Stretch:** Use hurdle, wall, or partner. Keep the raised leg straight and bent chest down toward knee.

8) **Way Backs:** Spread legs, bend over and reach as far back as possible between the legs. Do not allow legs to bend. Picture #2 is a variation.

9) **Knee pulls:** From lying position put left arm back and keep left leg extended. Right arm pulls right knee toward chest.

Lower Back Flexibility Drills

Many athletes have problems with their lower backs. Three good lower back exercises have been used for several years with much success. These were adapted from David Paris, a certified athletic trainer from Eugene, Oregon.

Assume the positions shown below. In sequence number two, the athlete tilts the pelvic area by pressing the stomach downward, trying to flatten the small of the back. An isometric contraction is then held from 6 to 10 seconds. To aid in the proper tilt, the chin is pressed down on the chest and the buttocks are tightened. Gradually do more and more of these. (See Illustration number 1 and number 2)

Another variation is to lift one knee toward the head. Then lift the other knee. Do this slowly. (Illustration number 3)

A final variation is to bring both knees toward the head. Again, do these slowly. (Illustration number 4)

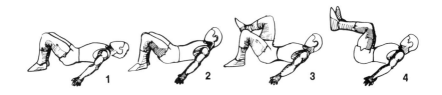

Plyometrics Drills

These are drills that can be used by all athletes to increase a more ballistic movement. They should be used more in pre-season than during the season.

Plyometrics are unique jumping exercises which contribute to the neuromuscular system in several ways. Most importantly, these exercises teach the neuromuscular system to react immediately to an overloaded muscle during the stretch reflex phase of muscular movement. (See Diagram #1)

Immediate reaction of muscles upon landing.

As the athlete lands under the force of his body weight and gravity, the muscles are pre-stretched prior to contracting to produce the next jump. A pre-stretched muscle reacts more explosively. This is one of the reasons plyometrics are superior to standing and jumping.

By conducting a plyometric program year round, the athlete's neuromuscular systems becomes accustomed to the demands of the ballistic movements—throwing, jumping, hurdling, and sprinting—and the body performs more efficiently during these movements. The speed movements of the leg muscles are directly related to basic running and stride pattern (push-off) and also related to each event during various phases of their unique techniques. These explosive reactions are a must in the field events, sprinting, and hurdling.

It is very important to include jumping drills in the training routine of all of the track and field athletes. The percentage of the training routine devoted to plyometrics varies according to the event's needs, but is included in all areas. Plyometrics bridge the gap between the absolute strength that is gained in the weight room and the ballistic strength involved in the actual execution of each event or movement. On one end of the strength training spectrum is the weight room and on the other end is the actual event.

Normal Weight Routine	Plyometrics bridge the gap and offer a blend of strength and the benefits of overload on a simulation of the exact movement found in the performance of the actual event.	Actual Event

In addition to bridging the gap, plyometrics also acts as a catalyst and seems to speed up development on both ends of the spectrum. Certainly the explosive events incorporate more emphasis on the area of plyometrics. However, outstanding improvements have been seen in ahtletes in all events largely through use of plyometrics as a small, but important part of the complete training of an athlete.

Physiologically, the muscle is best trained when following these guidelines: 1) the faster the muscle is forced to react, the greater the force that is applied, thus a greater training effect; 2) the athlete must continually be challenged (overload theory) for a training effect (more jumps, higher jumps); 3) adequate rest between sets (quality efforts stressed); 4) strength base is important before intense plyometrics are implemented (athletes are individuals and the coach must design appropriate levels of intensity); 5) plyometrics should be done no more than twice weekly in the off season and probably only once a week in season; 6) it is very important to start with only a limited amount of plyometric work and gradually increase in a progressive manner the number and volume of plyometric drills; 7) the larger boxes are more strength-power producing while the shorter boxes are more speed related. Research seems to say that boxes in the 0.75-meter range are speed boxes and boxes in the 1.15-meter range are for strength-power. We utilize boxes of 12 inches, 18 inches, 24 inches, 36 inches, 42 inches and 48 inches.

1) **Southern Cal Drill:**
   Athlete jumps up and down 18-inch box as quickly as possible for 15 to 30 seconds.

2) **Multiple Box Jumps:**
   Athlete jumps a series of boxes, all of which progressively increase in height.

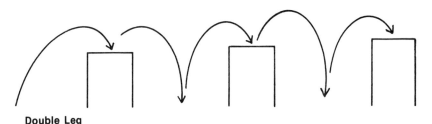

Double Leg

3) **Basic Depth Jump:**
   Athlete drops off large box of 42 inches and attempts to jump for height after hitting the ground. Both feet land simultaneously and explode upward.

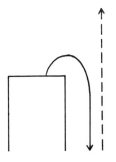

4) **Box Hops:**
   The athlete uses the small 12 inch box and hops through a series of small boxes. Only the lower leg and the ankle are used for the

hops. Alternate all right leg hops with left leg hops.

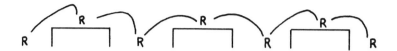

5) **Bounds:**
Bounds are exaggerated strides, and a slight gliding in the air occurs. The athlete exaggerates the forward-upward knee drive in rhythm with a double-arm action. Emphasis is on horizontal drive.

6) **Hops-One Legged Hops for 10 to 30 Yards:**
These are active hops when the hopping leg comes full circle with the heel almost touching the buttocks.

7) **Combos:**
A term used for any combination of hops and steps executed over 30 to 40 yards even up to 100 yards. Example would be: R-R-L-R-R-L-R-R-L or R-R-L-L-R-R-L-L
Simply a combination of successive hops and bounds.

8) **Stadium Bounds:**
Athlete bounds up stadium stairs using normal arm motion of sprinting while skipping every other step.

9) **Toe Bounces**
Hold a 40 pound barbell and bounce in sets of 25 repetitions. Exaggerate the toe push-off and the ankle extension. The lower leg does most of the work.

10) **Triple Jumping**
The athlete can actually do full triple jump; a short 6 to 9 stride triple jump; or a standing triple jump.

11) **Stadium Hops**
If a large stadium is available, do double or single leg hops up the stadium. It is best to walk down.

Sprint Drills

These are sprint drills because they mimic the sprint action, but they are good for teaching the ballistic muscle actions necessary for all athletic endeavors as well as for rhythm and coordination. Do them daily, year-round, with all athletes. These are valuable to proper sprint coaching.

SPRINT DRILLS:

In all of these drills, the emphasis is on staying tall. This position is as if someone was holding the athlete up slightly by the hair on his head. Never allow the hips to sink. All drills are done on the upper ball of the foot and toes.
A. **High Knee Action:** Stay tall and do not try to go too fast. These are bouncy, slower than normal slides. Emphasize an exaggerated knee lift, a slight extension of the lower leg on the down swing, and an explosive, bouncy drive off the big toe each time.
B. **Quick High Knee Action:** This is similar to the high knee action drill. In high knee action, the athlete has a long, bouncy, higher-than-normal knee action stride that is done at relatively slow speed. This drill involves running tall, while pumping the arms and knees with a quick, light up and down action. The forward speed is

not fast, but the action of arms and legs is quick. Knees should rise above the waist. Do not bend over with upper body.

C. **Backward High Knee Action:** The athlete runs backwards. Again he runs tall, lifts the knees high, and pushes backward. A slight backward lean is essential.

D. **Backward Spry's:** This is another backward running drill. In this drill, the athlete leans forward with the upper body and pushes backward. The backward run involves the forward leaning upper body and a bouncy stride, as the athlete pushes hard with the lower leg. Both backward runs use a different set of muscles than the forward runs.

E. **Butt Kicks:** Again start in a "running tall" position. All the action in this drill is in the arms and lower legs. The knees stay down and the athlete uses the lower leg to kick his buttocks with his heels. The buttocks kicking is very quick, but the forward speed is slow. Coordinate arms with the rhythm of the lower legs.

F. **Ashfords:** The arms dangle in front for balance and the athlete uses an exaggerated forward lean. A type of flutter kick run is begun. It is similar to the butt kick, but has more forward lean. The arms dangle in front for balance, and the heels do not come up to the buttocks area. The action is lower leg-oriented again and done very quickly.

G. **Skips:** This is an exaggeration of a normal skip. The athlete pushes off the grounded foot and drives the knee of the opposite leg up high. Arms are coordinated with the legs. These should be very rhythmic and explosive. On each skip, the ankle should be inside the knee of the leg off the ground and then snapped down to complete the skipping action.

H. **Kick Outs:** This is another version of the skip drill. As the athlete pulls the knee, he extends the lower leg in a "kick out" rather than a snap down. The heel comes under the buttocks, then extends.

Speed Endurance Drills

Speed endurance in the 100 and 200 is geared more to teaching the central nervous system not to tire. In the 400, it is known that glycogen stores are used up after 40 seconds. The runner must tolerate muscular functions in an acidic state—known in track vernacular as the bear jumping on the athlete's back.

There are several ways to improve speed-endurance. Three examples are:

1. Sets of fast repetitions. Use short rests between each repetition and longer rests between each set. This is consistent with research about training the sprint-energy systems. This is also a good time to teach correct start mechanics during the longer time between sets. An example of this drill is:
   a. 1-2 laps of striding the straights and walking the curves
   b. 3-5 X sprint starts—technique emphasis only—not for speed
   c. 2-4 X sprint starts—full speed—use commands and gun start (1-2 minute rest between repetitions. Three to five minute rest after the set is completed.
   d. 2-3 X 60 meter run from blocks using full commands and gun start (2-3 minute rest between each). Three to five minute rest after set is completed.
   e. 2-4 flying start 30's or 40's—1-2 minute rest between each
   f. Warm-down

2. Another version is to put the athletes' system through extended sprints that create oxygen debt. The athlete is allowed a long rest, but even with the rest his system is unable

27

to gain full recovery. He then forces his system into oxygen debt again. This process is repeated. The athlete learns not to lose form just because he is tired and in discomfort. His system learns to function in an acidic state. As the year progresses, the athlete can run faster and farther before he feels the "shutdown" effect of muscle acidity. This is beneficial to the 200 to 400 sprinter and the 400 meter hurdler. An example would be to run 3 X 352 yard run at 85% and 95% speed with 15 minutes walking recovery between each repetition.

3. A third variation is to run at 70 to 85 percent speed using a very short rest to deter recovery followed by another run at 70 to 85 percent. The pace isn't as fast but the short recovery soon puts the athlete into oxygen debt. An example is: 2 to 3 sets of a 300 meter run at 70 to 85 percent speed; quick walk for 100; 1 X 200 at 70 to 85 percent speed.

Similar drills for each of these can be used with the hurdlers using the appropriate size hurdle. Use the same drill except insert the sprint or intermediate hurdles.

High Energy Phosphate Drill

This drill is for both sprinters and hurdlers. The best training for high energy phosphates is 15 to 25 seconds at close to maximum speed with 2 to 3 minutes rest. This is a quality workout and is used primarily in season, but it can and should be used throughout the year. Three examples of this are:

1. Emphasize use of proper sprint form. The athlete runs a prescribed time (15 seconds as an example). The coach starts and stops the run with a signal. The athlete simply concentrates on a fast run using good sprint mechanics. Using 2 to 3 minute recoveries, the athlete does 5 to 8 repetitions of these.
2. Same philosophy as number one. Athlete runs 6 to 10 X 150 meters with 150 meter walk. This is good to use when the coach is unable to give complete supervision.
3. The same philosophy is behind this drill. Four X 200 meters at 400 meter race pace using a 2 to 3 minute rest recovery.

Race Awareness Drills

A. **100 Drill:** In this drill, stage a gradually accelerated run through a segmented lane. Demonstrate the stages in a 100 and what is probably going on at these distances in an actual race. Gradually accelerating instead of going full speed will allow the athlete to do several instead of one or two.

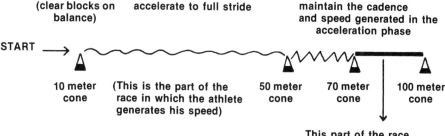

(clear blocks on   accelerate to full stride   maintain the cadence
balance)   and speed generated in the
                                                                 acceleration phase

START →

10 meter   (This is the part of the   50 meter   70 meter   100 meter
cone   race in which the athlete   cone   cone   cone
             generates his speed)

This part of the race
belongs to whomever slows
down the least. As odd
as this sounds, it is
documented by research.

As the athlete runs down the lane through the cones he thinks about each phase.

B. **200 Race Drill:** Split the 200's into phases so the athlete gets a visual awareness of what is happening in a perfectly run race. In 200 meter races when the first 100 was documented, the best 200 times come when the first 100 is closer to a personal record.

Put the first cone at 80 meters. The first 50 meters is very much like the first 50 in a 100. The athlete clears the blocks and accelerates. He cannot accelerate to full speed because this would adversely affect his later maintenance and deceleration phases. It must, however, be very close to full effort. Once an athlete reaches upright racing form, he cannot accelerate very much because his time on the surface with the driving leg is short. Therefore, proper early acceleration affects the entire race.

The reason the first cone is placed at 80 meters is that we want the athlete to get the neuro-muscular feeling of accelerating up to almost full speed and then carrying that speed through thirty more meters without either slowing down or trying to accelerate. The athlete does not run the 200 all at once. Instead, he runs a segment correctly, then walks back and starts the next segment. In this drill the next segment (cone) is a 60 meter section. This is a critical section because the athlete must learn to keep the acceleration gained in the first 80 meters. Key coaching words are: "maintain . . . don't press and don't slow down."

The athlete also must learn to make the transition from leaning on the curve to straight running. The major mistake is to pop-up immediately off the curve. This throws an unsteadiness into the 4 to 5 strides during this transition.

The last segment (cone) is again a maintenance phase where the athlete attempts to maintain the speed and cadence developed earlier. There will be some deceleration if the first segments were run as described, but if an athlete is aware of this and concentrates on his style and cadence he should not falter. More likely, he will appear to pull away. The key thoughts here are: "stay tall" and "keep hips up." Make sure that as soon as the foot drives off the track, it comes quickly *under* the buttocks. Carl Lewis's style is a good example of the technique to look for at this stage.

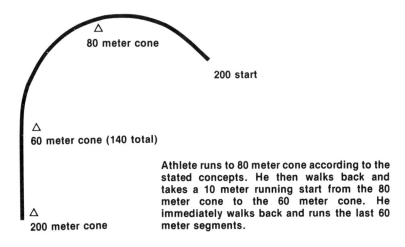

△
80 meter cone

200 start

△
60 meter cone (140 total)

Athlete runs to 80 meter cone according to the stated concepts. He then walks back and takes a 10 meter running start from the 80 meter cone to the 60 meter cone. He immediately walks back and runs the last 60 meter segments.

△
200 meter cone

C. **400 Meter Race Drill:** This follows the same pattern as the 200 drill. Run a segment, walk back, and run the next segment.

The segments (cones) are 80 meters, 160 meters, 80 meters and 80 meters.

The athlete comes out of the blocks and accelerates. In a 100 meter he accelerates to maximum; in a 200, slightly less; and the 400 is less than the 200, but certainly not casual. A top 400-meter runner will run the first 200 in about 21.5 to 22.7. The key to this segment is to accelerate and settle into pace or cadence.

The next coned-off area is 160 meters (240 total). During this phase, run to correct pace and cadence. Stay in the race and arrive past the 200 as close as possible to the planned 200 pace.

The next cone establishes another 80 meter segment. This is a critical segment because it covers the majority of the curve. A 400-meter runner must run the third 100 well since it is the curve. The athlete cannot slow down because it is very hard to generate it again. Fatigue is setting in and this is the place to keep a lead or close the gap if the athlete has allowed the early pace to be too slow. The athletes should feel like they are building speed into the curve even though they are actually maintaining or slow-

30

ing down slightly. The athlete also must learn to make the transition from curve running with a lean to straight running in an upright posture—just like in the 200 race drill.

The last segment is 80 meters. The concept to be learned here is exactly like the last 60 meters in the 200 drill.

In summary, the athlete runs a segment, walks back, and runs the next segment (1 x 80, 1 x 160, 1 x 80, 1 x 80 = total 400).

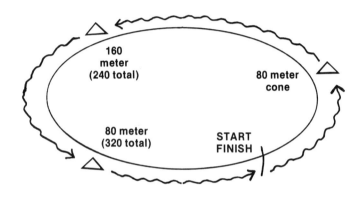

Start Drills

It is important to emphasize quality and concentration in drilling the start. The majority of start work should be done with a gun and the use of proper commands. Everything should be done to simulate meet conditions. It is best to only take a few starts during a practice session. High hurdlers should always use at least two high hurdles during start practice. Intermediate hurdlers should use one or two hurdles. Sprinters should cover 30 meters most of the time, and once in a while use starts while wearing spikes over 60 meters.

After each start, the coach and athlete should discuss what the athlete did or did not do relative to technique and philosophy. If possible, these starts should be video taped and reviewed.

For those with a low budget, the coach can make a starting gun by putting two boards on a hinge with handles on the outside of each board. This forms what is called a clap-board. The two boards, clapped together, make a sound much like that of a gun.

REACTION STARTS

Since quick reaction to a command is part of good starting, it is good to use a variety of stimuli as the command and not just the gun sound. One method is for the coach to gently place his hand on the back of the front leg in the middle of the hamstring. The athlete starts once he feels you release the tension on the hamstring. This also focuses the total concentration on the importance of an explosive reaction from the front leg. Another method is for the coach to kneel slightly to the side and front of the athlete. The athlete starts once the coach drops any small object, such as a key chain.

Touch
Here—Release
To Start

LEAN DRILL

This drill can be done at the end of the 100 meter race drill or as a separate drill. The purpose is to teach the athlete when and how to lean. Most video or film reviews of races show the athletes leaning too soon, and often improperly. Proper lean can only help .01-, .02- or .03-seconds, but this small amount increasingly becomes the difference between winning and placing.

The correct finish technique is to run through the line. Always lean when a foot is in contact with the ground and then lean at the last moment. The proper lean is shown in this picture—arms back and body bent at the waist.

A video of this drill is beneficial to the athlete.

Neuro-Muscular Speed Drills

SURGICAL TUBE DRILL

There are commercial products that can be purchased, but it is possible to buy ¾ inch surgical tubing in 50 foot lengths. Attach a cloth belt to both ends. This produces an apparatus that allows the runner to run out against resistance while the partner stands still, creating the resistance on the tubing. By stretching the tubing against resistance, the athlete improves both drive and power. He then becomes stationery and his partner runs toward him. The tubing has been stretched and as he runs toward the partner who ran away, he is able to run faster than normal because of the assistance of the tubing. This is a great over-speed drill. It teaches the neuro-muscular system to adjust to a slightly faster stride. The athlete can repeatedly run fast without much fatigue.

ACCELERATIONS

The athlete thinks about proper sprint form. Start slowly using good sprint mechanics and gradually increasing speed. A good way to insure progressive acceleration is to gauge the arm tempo and attempt to gradually make the arms move through a quicker and quicker cycle. The athlete should move from standing still up to 80 percent speed and to maintain it in a relaxed, controlled manner. After holding the 80 percent speed a second or two, he then gradually decelerates.

VARIATED SPEED RUNS

Varied speed runs should be used in season. These can be the normal acceleration runs which move from a standstill up through the entire range of the athlete's speed. Another version is to accelerate - relax - accelerate. The variety is endless and is the product of the coach's imagination. These are important because current research seems to indicate that constantly changing intensities produces a "speed change" more quickly than exercises that involve only a steady speed.

WHISTLE DRILL
This drill is used with the sprint drills or as a varied run drill. The coach uses a whistle or command to change the athlete from one movement to another.

EXAMPLES
Before the start of the drill, the coach tells the athlete to start with high knee action; a command to change to quick high-knee drill; at the next command to change to butt kicks. The athlete is continually moving and changes at the whistle-command. The coach's imagination is the only limit to the varieties that can be used.

A second way the whistle/command drill can be used is as a version of the varied speed drill. Before the run, the coach sets the various speeds on whistle; change back to jog on next whistle. Or, it could involve these changes on command: jog; high knee; stride; sprint; back to jog until the coach stops the session. Again, the coach's imagination is all that limits how many changes, what type, and how long. It is a good change from normal workouts.

BAREFOOT RUNS AND HILL RAMPS RUNS
These are two drills used to strengthen the sprint muscles: quadricepe, plantarflexors, and dorsiflexors.

Neglected areas to be worked are lower foot and leg strength. At full speed, the athlete supports and balances the entire body on the ball of one foot. In America, shoes are worn from birth and this often creates atrophied foot muscles because the shoe acts as a cast. Special attention should be given to this problem. By doing some running on grass, you can strengthen the foot, lower leg, and the achilles tendon which aids in the snap of the foot off the ground into the tight buttock position found in proper sprint recovery.

The second drill is incline or hill running. This requires a more forceful drive off the lower leg and taxes the quadriceps. Ramps in a football stadium that are inclined 30 degrees can be used. Any similar hill can also be used: drive up and walk down.

Relay Drills

STANDING BATON DRILL
Four to six athletes stand in a line. The baton will be passed right hand to left; left to right; right to left, down the line. People can

interchange positions to learn to take the pass with either hand. The receiving hand will come back high and palm up. The passer must look into the palm as he extends his baton hand out by placing the free end of the baton in the open palm. This is done on an oral command. Once a team is established, they will stand in the same order they will run in the meet.

This drill can also be done while the group jogs around the track. This forces the athletes to concentrate more because the hand-off occurs while the hands are moving. This more closely relates to the actual relay hand-off.

WARM-UP HAND-OFFS—CONTINUOUS RELAY

Station five runners at each sprint relay exchange zone. A mark of 12 to 15, heel-toe steps is placed at each position. All runs are at half-speed. Runner number one hands to number two right hand to left hand. Runner one then stays at the exchange point and waits for the baton to go around the track. Runner two, with the baton in the left hand, passes to number three's right hand. Number two stays at that position. Number three continues the relay by handing off to four's left hand, and after the hand-off remains at that station. Number four continues the run and hands off left to right to five. Number five begins another time around the track. The relays continue until five is back at his original position.

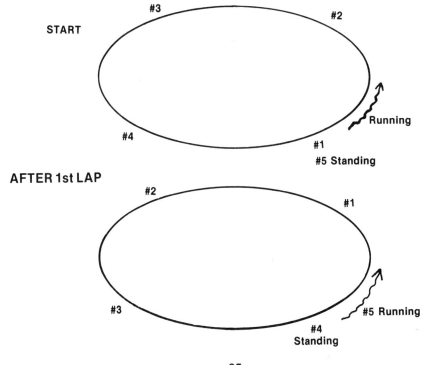

The next lap would look like this

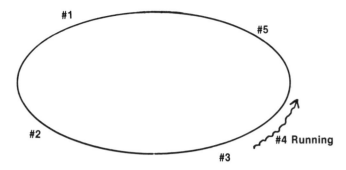

MOVING SPRINT RELAY DRILL
   The athletes work in pairs on either the straight or curves. They run at a quick, but controlled pace. The incoming runner puts the baton into the outgoing man's hand as many times as he can during 100 meters. The outgoing man never completely receives the baton. When the baton hits his palm he wraps around it and releases. The incoming runner maintains control of the baton at all times. This teaches the ability to execute the baton pass while moving.

Beginner Hurdle Drills

These drills are good for young athletes learning to hurdle.
RUBBER-TOPPED HURDLE: A large sheet of foam rubber is cut and stapled to one side of the wooden cross bar of an old hurdle. It is then folded over and stapled to the other side of the cross bar to create a 6-inch fold above the wooden cross bar.

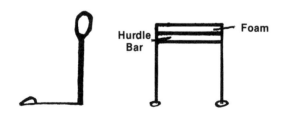

With a 6-inch foam fold for the topping, the coach can place the hurdle at 30 inches and have a 36 inch height to clear. A 36 inch setting also produces 42 inches to clear. The benefit of this apparatus is that the foam fold topping takes away the fear and frees the youngster to learn correct hurdle technique. It looks like a real hurdle and can be adjusted up and down like one, but it will not scare or hurt the hurdle prospect. It is best to make three of these foam rubber hurdles. As the athlete learns to hurdle, the coach should remind him that when he feels a "hit" against the foam that this will be wood or plastic on the "real" hurdle. Don't let them become complacent and hit the foam everytime.

STICKS AND BRICKS: Another good way to introduce novices to hurdling is to place bricks or wooden blocks with a thin wooden stick—yardstick or the thin ceiling or floor boarder material—at various low heights. If the athlete hits the stick, it falls to the ground. As with the foam rubber hurdle, this drill takes the fear out of the exercise. This drill is good with youngsters because the height of the "stick and brick" is very low. A wide variety of hurdles can be made by stacking blocks or standing them on end. The stick just lies across the blocks to form the hurdle.

 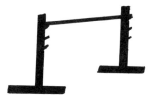

GRASS HURDLING: This is another good way to teach a beginning hurdler. Place the hurdles on the grass so that the fear of falling is lessened. Keep the hurdle very low and set it up so the athlete can get three steps between each hurdle. Gradually move the hurdles farther apart and gradually raise the height. Once the athlete masters hurdling on the grass, he can then move to the track for correct spacing and height.

HURDLING THROUGH A WINDOW: This drill teaches the athlete to get proper lean on top of the hurdle. Use a broken cross bar or thin stick and hold it about 2 to 3 feet above the hurdle. The athlete must then dip his upper body and head to keep from hitting the cross bar.

TRAIL LEG—HIP CIRCLES
The athlete leans against a fence or something similar. He then practices the full trail leg movement. The foot rotates outward, opening the hip joint, and the knee cycles through. At the highest point in the circle, the knee of the trail leg will almost touch the arm pit.
Another variation is to add a hurdle to cycle over.

As the athlete becomes more proficient, he can speed up the movements.

SIDE HURDLE DRILLS

In each of these variations, the athlete sets the hurdles at the correct height and correct spacing. He then emphasizes either the lead leg or the trail leg action. Instead of hurdling down the center of the hurdle, he "cheats" by only clearing half the hurdle. If he is emphasizing the lead leg, then it goes over the hurdle but the trail leg comes "outside" the hurdle and doesn't have to clear anything. The other variation is to emphasize the trail leg action by placing the lead leg outside the hurdle, clearing nothing, and bringing the trail leg over the half of the hurdle. This isolates each action and allows the athlete to focus on one thing at a time.

HURDLE SKIPS

The hurdles are placed very close together (2 to 3 yards in most cases).The rhythm of this drill is: skip-step-skip-step. The skip is explosive, with the knee driven high. The entire lead leg goes over the 30 inch hurdle. The lead leg stays bent in a normal skipping fashion. This teaches rhythm and the very important concept of leading with a bent knee before extending.

LOW HURDLES

A great drill for sprinters and hurdlers is the old high school 180 yard low hurdles race. The coach can use the full 180 yards or portions of it to create the workout. In this drill, the hurdles are placed 20 yards apart and 30 inches high. For women, the spacing is adjusted to a distance that would require seven strides. The athlete uses a seven stride pattern. This teaches even striding for the sprinter. For the hurdler, the emphasis is on speed and a proper bent knee lead leg action.

SPEED HURDLE DRILL
   This drill emphasizes speed, quick rhythm, and the concept of leading with the knee for the hurdle clearance. The hurdles are spaced by placing them on the women's hurdle mark for men and much closer for women. This makes the three step cadence come easily and quickly. The hurdles are set at lower than normal heights. For men, this is either 30-, 33-, or 36-inches. For women, it is 24- or 30-inches. The low height makes clearance very easy and frees the mind to really concentrate on technique at a fast pace. The low height and close spacing allows the athlete to focus on a properly bent lead knee prior to extension and to also get the neuro-muscular feeling of a quick, rhythmic, sprint through the hurdles.

   It is best to train the hurdlers with sprinters. The hurdler is a sprinter first and foremost. Here are some high hurdle drills as part of a conditioning workout:

QUICKNESS
   1. 12 HH-12-yards apart: take five steps between and emphasize quickness over the hurdle.
   2. 12 HH—8 to 9 yards apart: emphasis is on quickness over the hurdle. Take three steps between.
   3. 14 hurdle drill: a version of the above that combines the quick-ness drill and the development of endurance is the placing of hurdles 8 to 9 yards apart. Run as a full flight. The distance to the first hurdle is kept at 15 yards the same as a normal high hurdle race.

ENDURANCE AND QUICKNESS OVER THE HURDLE
   Five hurdles facing one way in one land and five hurdles facing opposite direction in the next lane. This is endurance hurdling.

Run down through five hurdles, turn around and come back immediately through the other five. Rest and repeat. The hurdles are spaced 10 to 12 yards apart and the athlete takes five steps between. This can also be done 9 to 10 yards apart with three steps.

TECHNIQUE
It is often good to spend an entire workout just emphasizing a different aspect of hurdle technique and working until it has been satisfactorily improved.

Hurdle Race Drills

INDOOR MEET DRILLS
Work with a gun start over 5 to 7 hurdles. These are basically full speed. Do them in sets. An example is to run 1 X 5 hurdles full and to walk immediately back and repeat. Rest about three minutes and repeat. Always sprint off the last hurdle. This is a very good drill to video tape and analyze. Occasionally, the athlete should run the full flight three to five times with about ten minutes of rest between. Caution should be used as to when and how many of these are done.

400-METER HURDLE RACE DRILLS
Simulating hurdling while tired and then learning the difference in the feelings involved in the different segments of the race are accomplished by these drills. These also help in pace and step-pattern. The word flat means no hurdles in that segment.

Each of these workout drills is used in conjunction with the proper warm-up/hurdle drills: side and lead leg exercise, followed by weights or plyometrics, and a cool down.

WORKOUT NUMBER ONE: First 200 over IH, four to six times at race pace. The athlete comes out of the blocks and runs the first 200 of a normal 400 hurdle race. He is timed at touch down over each hurdle to check proper pace. The coach also observes the technique and step pattern and makes corrections as necessary. This drill is done 4 to 6 times at the athlete's race pace. The rest interval is usually a 200-meter walk.

WORKOUT NUMBER TWO: First 200 meters flat and go into the last 5 hurdles—total of a 400 half flat, half hurdles, at four times. The athlete will run 400 meters a total of four times. In this drill, half of the 400 has no hurdles and half of it has five intermediate hurdles set at normal 400 hurdle spacing. The athlete runs the first 200 flat at a comfortable pace. He then goes right into the last five hurdles using race pace and correct race step pattern. He learns to attack the hurdles in the curve while tired as well as learning the feeling of the last segment of the race.

WORKOUT NUMBER THREE: First 3 IH like race—stride flat backstretch—and go immediately into the last 3 IH—total 400 (at 4). This is an easy way to teach the start and early step pattern as well as teaching the capability of adjusting and attacking the last three hurdles without the previous step pattern.

WORKOUT NUMBER FOUR: 300 IH at pace—2 to 3 times. These are run like a race. They are timed at each hurdle to check pace and to emphasize the need to exaggerate the aggression and intensity from hurdle five to hurdle seven. This is an anaerobic workout and a full rest is needed between each one.

WORKOUT NUMBER FIVE: Run 150's or 200's and put in a hurdle for them to adjust to and to hurdle. It can help to place a small piece of tape at the correct takeoff point so he can adjust easier. This should eliminate the mistake of stutter-stepping.

WRONG LEG—STUTTER-STEP DRILL
This is a 400-meter hurdle drill which can be used with other sprint drills to complete a full workout.

All intermediate hurdlers should learn to hurdle efficiently with each leg. Two primary reasons for this are:

1. Most hurdlers must change their stride pattern as they get tired. A two-step change is too drastic. By alternating, the athlete only has a one-step adjustment.
2. Very often fatigue sets in at different hurdle segments. This means a quick thinking adjustment will be made regarding which leg comes as the lead leg. It often occurs that a hurdle that is hit will put the hurdler off-stride and also force an adjustment.

This drill simply involves all types of hurdling and other hurdle drills using the "wrong" lead leg. It is good to place an intermediate hurdler at various spacing so the athlete must adjust and clear the hurdle without slowing down. Place a piece of tape on the track at the correct takeoff point for the athlete to see.

This could mean running a normal interval workout with a hurdle placed randomly in the run. The athlete has to see the barrier and to adjust his stride pattern with only a minimum amount of slowing down. It should be clear that this also teaches the ability to lead with either leg. The variations of this are many. A more systematic version of this drill is to place a hurdle at each 100-meter mark and to run a workout that involves repeat 400's or repeat segments of the 400.

As part of the workout, include timed runs over only the first three intermediate hurdles for pace and stride pattern. These are important hurdles because if the athlete gets step and rhythm early, he is less likely to have problems later in the race. The ability to maintain momentum is extremely important to great 400 meter hurdling. This is one of the reasons a rhythmic, consistent stride pattern is so necessary. With 400 meters and 10 hurdles to cover, the athlete cannot afford to be off much. An athlete, off only 29 inches per stride over a 15-stride pattern will change his hurdle takeoff point 30 inches which creates a problem in clearance. To maintain momentum and stride pattern, the athlete must run slightly toward the outside of the lane.

Because of the physiological energy demands and the importance of maintaining speed, it is important that the athlete be able to hurdle with either leg, or to be tall enough and fit enough to maintain 13 strides all the way. Edwin Moses has popularized the 13-step pattern, but remember that Mike Shine, the 1976 Olympic silver medalist, ran: 48.6 using 15 steps all the way.

CONCLUSION

The great value of drills is that they isolate a specific section of the event. This allows the athlete to focus all mental and emotional forces on learning the specific movements isolated by the drill.

Consistent, correct use of drills enables the athlete's neuro-muscular system to create a "groove." The pattern that develops then stays with the athlete even during the times of greatest stress. Once a correct pattern becomes natural through these repeated sessions, the athlete will see improvements.

The secret to the correct use of drills in training is to be consistent and to repeat the proper movement. It is important to realize that practice does not make perfect, practice makes permanent. Therefore, perfect practice makes perfect. Not only must the athlete repeat these, but he must also attempt to be a perfectionist in his approach. The watchful eye of a trusted coach is critical.